Looking Inward

Modeste Herlic
Sarah Lima

Author's edition
2nd Edition
2023

Looking Inward

Translated by Modeste Herlic

For those who wonder about their inner life.

When fear troubles your mind
and there is no other way out,
turn away from remorse,
open your heart,
close your eyes,
and wait without wanting anything.
Right there,
your Inner Truth will sing the most beautiful song
when your mind has stopped talking.

***

A flower

I see a flower
because I am a flower
I see pain
because I am in pain
I project outwardly what I am within
In this eternal cinema of existence
my being is a writer, actor, and designer

***

Today

I trust the universe
I enjoy every moment
Far from fear
I spend the day in contentment
I smile at the changes
I am grateful
I give thanks
I take a deep breath
My heart is calm

***

Surrender

I do not need to do everything on my own
I can stop now
and listen to the advice
the spirit guides
reflected in the voice of my intuition

***

What if I took a closer look at the world?

8

I passed by many beautiful things
without being able to look at them.
How many wonders has my gaze missed?
The most beautiful things in the world
wait beside me to be perceived.

Today I will open my eyes
speak, serene
walk, calmly
and realize what is necessary

***

It is today, it is now

He who puts off love until tomorrow
lives in a great lie
"Leave it for tomorrow"
is an illusion of the mind
Today and now
I begin the journey of love
If I wait until I am ready
the boat of happiness
will leave me behind

***

What I do when I get lost

When the thousand paths of earth are confused,
and I can no longer discern my task in the chaos,
I turn my eyes to the sky
and contemplate the non-manifest.
Thus, through the indigo face,
I recognize the path of paths,
the ultimate route that leads to serenity.

***

Where does life take place?

In the details
in the details
when I surrender
to the little moments
That is when life happens

***

Detachment

The suitcase with the old clothes,
even the especially beautiful ones,
must one day be gone
so that a new cycle can begin
so that I can walk
in the garden of Beauty
with a new outfit
a colorful robe

***

I take care of my day

I do not make my day
a rush of misfortunes
I am serene
I am calm
I meditate
Every moment
I caress my day
with thoughts of joy

***

A new look

Expectations are meant to be broken
A new perspective can be created
at any moment of the day

***

Once upon a time

In the deep black of the sky,
the stars came together like a garland of flowers.
They beamed on me with all their love and sang,
"Hear! Hear! When you become king of yourself,
we will be your crown."
O how happy I was at this moment.
"Yes, I will. Yes, I will. I will be king of myself," I
sang softly.
And the whole landscape became a symphonic jewel.

***

A natural law

"Everything goes,
comes back and renews"
This I must understand
to avoid suffering

***

I accept life as it is

I forgive the adversities
So, I allow my heart
to swim joyfully in calm waters
That is how I speak of hope again

***

Happiness

Happiness is when I am still
and contemplate life,
which dies with every sunset
and renews itself with every dawn

***

A good question

From where I stand,
I see the opulent man
being dragged impetuously away
by the angel of death.
The dying man looked back sadly,
for he realized how insignificant his gold was.
Now I ask myself,
"Why am I working so hard to be rich?"

***

I hide a lotus in my pocket

When they say my body is dirty
I listen with a smile and go on my way
for it is well known
that the lotus is the son of the swamp

***

The best way

Life's journey seems long
and many paths deceive.
But in the heart,
there is a happy way.
Why do I not look there, to my inner self?

***

A definition of life

For a long time, I have watched existence
and did not see its light.
I have listened to it
and did not hear its song.
As today is the day of new beginnings,
I close my eyes for a moment.
I take a deep breath,
deep into the depths of the soul.
I breathe in and out, softly, and gently.
I release myself from my fears,
my old beliefs, and limitations.
Then, through the vision of the heart,
I realize that life is a learning experience.

***

When I choose to change

I recognize in myself
the ability to overcome any obstacle.
I have the gift to heal my wounds,
either by meditating deeply
or by asking for help.
Either way, I will take control of my life.

***

A feather

What is true is light,
flowing like a joyful river
Today I choose to be a feather
that takes off with a single breath
Today I choose to be a dancer
who rises to the sky
and dances with the golden star

***

The song of the wind

The chattering mind,
detached from the soul,
tries to convince me of everything,
keeping me in a perpetual race
with what is illusory.
Fortunately,
I can hear my heart each night
as I lie down
and listen to the song of the wind:
"You are not the fool
You are not the mind
You are not the vassal
You are the master
You are the one
who watches the mind."

***

The most perfect garden

I go there to stroll
in the garden of Today.
I want to delight
in the fragrance of the Now.
How gentle are the whispers of each moment!
How beautiful are the flowers of each breath!
The illusion of the mind is far from me.
I can water the plants of wisdom in peace.
So I walk with slow steps.
Patience is my sword.
Patience is my shield.
Then I walk cheerfully
with a smile on my lips

***

I must understand

Rejecting adversity
does not reduce hardship.
When I view adversity
as an opportunity for growth,
I can give a different meaning
to my experiences

***

A change

Shifting from "thinking" to "observing"
can change my entire perspective.

***

The Muses

Have you ever observed yourself like this?
In doubt between living or running
receiving or giving
possessing or being…
Many questions are a waste of time
I want to lie down, be still
And wait …
Wait and wait
Until the muses of patience
come and sing "LOVE" into my ears

***

I get to know myself

When I observe myself,
I compare the before with the now,
I see maturation and love.
But this happens
only when I see myself.
Because most of the time,
I turn away from myself.

***

The harm I do to myself

In the effort of avoiding the unknown,
I deprive myself of contact with the Divine
that dwells within me.

***

Always ready for a new beginning

If what I have experienced until now
has not gladdened my heart
I must waste no more time,
I must adjust the sails
and recalculate the routes.
Life is an eternal movement.

***

Gratitude

I am grateful
for who I am
and for what I have
Every day
my inner world invites me
to look into my soul
and see my greatness

***

I let life surprise me

When my body is full of fear
Everything becomes repetitive and boring
Life loses all its grace
Sadness covers up my beauty
My day gets lost in the restlessness
"No, no"
Today I say "no" to fears
I want to breathe and dream
I wish to sing and dance
with delicate movements
and a body as light as a rose

***

A gift

Presently,
the greatest blessing,
is me stumbling.
I want to hit the ground
and spill the certainties
that have already taken hold.
I hope to make room
for the revolution
that life wanted to bring me.

***

What the soul wants

Many people pray to God
asking for material things
or giving thanks
for what they have received
But a free soul only wants
to play a golden lute
for the stars that lie
like lotuses in the sky

***

A definition of love

The whole of human existence
is nothing but the Sublime Love
that unites man to himself, and to his neighbor.
This same love cares for Mother Earth,
and delights the souls of its human,
animal, and vegetable children.
Love connects people
and makes the world a better place to live.

Let us love, my friends
The sea of happiness is infinite
Let us plunge into this pleasure
and wet our minds and bodies
with everlasting joy

***

Another definition of Love

Between the extremes,
Love is the path of truth.
It is the sweet flute of the Soul
that plays when we lose our way,
calling us back,
pulling us off the shoulder.

***

I trust myself

I do not give up my self-love
which is blue and endless
as an ocean that covers
my inmost being

I can still do so much
waltz with my joy
smile at strangers
walk in victory
go out with friends
In fact,
I have many Love grapes
to offer the world

***

I want to love

When I give up the preconceived ideas,
the convinced certainties,
the suspicious looks
and the proud speech,
then I am ready to receive the love of the universe
Then I am ready to become the universe

***

How can I love?

I have suffered much trying to learn something
that cannot be taught.
Now I know:
"You only learn to love by loving"

***

The wind of kindness

This energy
that blows among beings
with good hearts
has passed through me,
and through you,
a hundred times,
and will continue.
Whenever any of us forgets it,
it will remind us again.

***

The cycle of good deeds

In the end
it all begins again
There will always be
another opportunity
to do good,
to do right,
to banish the lie from our lives

***

Acceptance

By allowing myself
to be who I am
I accept the other person
And I give her
the gift of being who she is

***

My truth

By exchanging "reason" for "compassion",
I find a goddess within me.

***

What am I?

"You are Love, for only Love creates.
It is you, who shapes your pain and your joy,"
answered my heart.

***

Our mission

Sometimes life presents itself like a knot
that needs to be untied.
We are the only ones who can do it.
Because there is no way
to delegate our happiness
to a third party.

***

A consideration

The neophyte in life who walks the earth,
before he understands the world,
must know himself.

***

When all is gone,
and there is nothing left to give,
what you give for courage
is precious as gold
and full as moonlight.
So I act with my heart,
and turn my back on judgment.

***

A jewel of love

A smile is a rose
that a soul gives to another.

***

I

I am a soul
immeasurable
unlimited
an infinite sea
trapped in clay

***

I AM

No one is born ready
That is what they say
But deep inside
there is nothing to become
There is nothing to do
Just TO BE
And I already AM
All that is left
is to remember ME

***

The good direction

Outside,
the restless mind
makes me feel nothing
From within,
delicate and silent fireflies
show me the path

***

In my heart

Deep, light, and infinite
This is the being
that inhabits my heart
This is the being that I AM

***

The eyes of the soul

In the painting of Eternity, the colors are different, but the creation is one. In the same way, the Painter is ONE. His ink is called "Divine Essence" and can only be seen through the eyes of the soul, through the "observer" who loves.

***

To my friend

The light you see in the sun,
the light you see in others
radiates from you.
So look in the mirror,
with compassion
as if you were doing it
for the first time
and you will see Love

***

Know how to appreciate

It's the little things
that comfort the soul
The smallest details,
those little things
only when I stop to breathe,
they are revealed to me
In the magic of appreciation
of every moment
of every smile
every hug
every gesture

***

Why do I walk so much?

Who has never thought about running?
On the other hand, who has ever asked herself,
"What am I running from?"
At some point, I must look inward, accept, and
surrender.

***

Inward

I asked the old man,
"If there were a path that would satisfy all my deepest
doubts, would I follow it?"
The man replied nonchalantly,
"There is only one, and it leads inward."

***

My secret in a moment of unrest

When I stop the bustle of the day
and surrender to the unknown
I feel the silent but screaming pulsating waves
that dance from side to side
ambiguous and perfectly connected
in the fullness of my being

***

About the I

The Soul that I AM,
calls for a feast
IT is not lukewarm
IT loves to dance and sing
IT is there in the universe
inside or outside the body
hidden or revealed
IT is pure expansion

***

At the core of being,
there is nothing
that distinguishes it from others.

***

About us

Every being is a glass of water
that is full by itself
He who believes he is one half
has not yet truly seen himself

***

When I look at what troubles me with innocent eyes, as
if it were the first time, I realize the openness of the
soul that I AM.

***

As I ponder,
something subtle
resonates within me,
"Come here! Come here!
Come into your heart
Come into the moment
Be present here and now
And see your problems with clarity."

***

The questioning

At the end of the eternal search, you have found nothing, as if everything you have done was worth nothing.

I go on and on. With each step forward, I fall behind and see the memory of what I have learned fading.

Maybe I need to do everything the other way around:
"Stop forever
Stop moving
Look where I have never looked before
Whistle with the birds
Lie under a starry sky
Breathe deeply
Sing with the night and sleep in peace."

***

The attention

I let the first breath of morning caress my face
I rejoice, unpretentiously, when I see the plant in the
garden
I ruffle the ends of my hair as I hold my pen to write
A smile curls my lips as I feel life coursing through my
body
It is time to write letters of love on a golden paper

***

The purpose

I spend a lot of time worrying about the meaning of my
life. However, I speak in singular, "my purpose."
Why must I have only one? In a world so vast, where
there are many people, where there are such
wonderfully hidden places, and where there are so
many lands never explored before. Why do I need only
one destination?
Why should I have to conform?
Why not live without boundaries?

***

I could not even imagine it.
How could I?
Reasonable, thoughtful, rational, but there is no escape
from what comes from within.
What arrives unexpectedly and takes over the room,
blinding the eyes of those who were not prepared to see
all that sprouts there.
O, that is so beautiful, it silences me.

***

Controlling things is not for me

I cannot control my days with all my powers.
Maybe I could do it with some hope.
But many circumstances get me down.
They remind me that the control I have over things…
"Control?"
Did I think I had any control?

***

Unity

The rain that rejuvenates the world refreshes the body
and renews the mind. The rain is but one thing. And
yet, as I watch it silently from my window, I see a
legion of water drops, each one incomplete and
complete at the same time.

The thunder sings
and I listen:
"You are the rain
You are a drop of water
You are the rain
You are a drop of water
Big and small
Big and small"

***

I am not alone

What do I know of love?
What do I know of infinity?
What do I know of the world?
I am dust before immensity
I am a zeptosecond before eternity
But I have something here inside me
I have this heat that drives me on
I have that sublime particle
that connects me to every spark of the universe
That is the reason I am not alone

***

Day and night, all one thing. And you who recognize
this have a keen eye for the enjoyment of the elixir of
divine beauty.

***

I must rest

I do not have to go very far
I am only a breath away from my destiny
from the essence that connects me to everything

***

The deepest desire of my heart is no secret
It has been revealed to me before
and a million times over
I have known it
But I have forgotten
So I must come home and find myself

***

"We are lights on the same path
divine particles with the same goal
You may not remember now
But it is all within you
See how cracks open inside you
and rays of light come out
when you are happy
That's the way it is."

***

Another interpretation of Unity

The drop of water
which has the spirit of the sea
means nothing
until it has mingled
with thousands of its kind
and become the sea itself,
immeasurable and infinite.

I really want to reclaim my greatness
But first,
I must unite with my fellow men

***

From solitude

Solitude should not be feared
In it, I see myself
In it, we are ME and all the other versions of me

***

How beautiful it is
to feel the tenderness of life

Sweet is the breeze that reminds me that I am not alone.
It caresses my body and soul with messages from
infinity and restores the connection between me and the
spiral of love.

***

What I know about Dharma

All I wanted was life
as I had imagined it
Nothing more, nothing less
But who said life would take my wishes
at the reincarnation switch?

***

O my friend
the effort may seem right
But remember
To form the puzzle
the pieces fit together naturally
as if they spent a lifetime
looking for each other

***

Surrender

When I feel like giving up, I remind myself that there is a perfect order that takes care of everything. All it needs, is for me to get out of its way, and let it do its thing.

***

There is a great friend within

As night fell, the inner voice whispered to me,
"Another day of testing has been won."
At dawn, the same melody caressed me,
"Only lift your eyes, for today I am your wings."

***

An event

One day, I went to the Garden of Silence and sat down under the Tree of Redemption. I closed my eyes and sang "h-u-u-u-u-u-u" with the wind, breathing in and out slowly and softly, moving my lips gracefully.

At some point I heard a mysterious voice saying, "You have never opened your eyes to face me and so hear the heavenly song that delights with the melody of love, the symphony that never fades."

This message was the most beautiful sound I had ever heard. Right after, I lay down in the soft grass and slept like a baby.

***

The universe

The blue screen above our eyes
with smoky white streaks
the living art of creation
specially created for us
day by day
a new painting
made with perfection
made with infinite love
the living art of creation
awaits our appreciation

***

O great star

I am fascinated by the sun
or envious of it
Maybe it's because it never gives up
It always comes to me
But I, on the other hand…

***

What is the benefit of duality?

Light and shadow
Peace and euphoria
I only know one
Because the other exists
All within me

***

There is no end without a beginning
A bad guy without a good guy
Hell without heaven
Black without white
Good without evil
Happiness without sadness
In the face of eternal duality,
one must awaken and accept it

***

Harmony

Among all possible times and universes, Creation wanted us to be here and now, sharing our lives with each other.

***

Being aware

When I notice there is something wrong with me
I project it outward and see something wrong in the
world
This interrupts my connection with the Divine
which connects me to all things

***

The universe is always waiting for me to reciprocate
It knows me and calls me by name
Whenever I listen
to the chirping of the birds

***

I have never been alone
The Universe walks in my shadow
Little by little, I am learning to trust It

One step back
is not a step back
It's not giving up
It's just a step back
to think
to see from afar
to breathe
And above all
to let life take its course

***

When all is still
when I am without direction
I take a step back to gain momentum
to give space to the Universe
not to stand in its way
That's how the untamed power lifts me up

***

When I let it happen

When I stop fighting and accept what is presented to
me as it is, something magical happens,
"The surrender to life
the trust in the path
the certainty of light after darkness."

***

How nice it is to open your hands, and relax a little
Especially when what is planned does not come to pass.

When I open my hands,
I feel the breeze
gently flowing between my fingers
When I open my hands,
I see the paths that I have walked
When I open my hands,
The tension of the grip disappears
I breathe
Deep
I calm down
And rejoice
And smile
All because I opened my hands

***

I have understood that there is no point in fighting my
feelings

The emotions move in my chest
like the energies that move in the universe
To stop the flow of my emotions
is to stop the river of my existence

***

A thought

Although a being is individual and unique, it is no different from a grain of sand in the desert or a drop of water in a vast ocean.

***

What I feel when I accept my immensity

84

I am a happy soul and resemble The Highest when I love and care for the surrounding beings.

***

A new resolution

After suffering much and facing the waves of life, I
concluded,
"The course of the river reflects the dance of life.
So from now on, I will be a river
and go with an open heart
to the Sea of Tranquilly.
There is my true home."

***

**The following is what I thought after a long day of
contemplation:**

I see the people around me, and I love them all, just as
I love the Creator — the one who, long ago, drew the
golden letters of love on my left chest.
O beautiful people, brothers and sisters, look within
yourselves, and notice the luminous words engraved
there forever.

***

Perfect action in inaction

I allow observation to be perfection.
There are moments when "doing nothing"
 is the only necessary action.

***

Where my self-love begins

In the magic of uncertainty
hides the sublime treasure
the power to listen to my inner self
to learn to trust myself
to accept and look at myself
with compassion and sympathy
with self-love

***

Time

This time here is light, fleeting, elusive
It should not catch my attention
My attention should be on what remains
what remains in the breath
that pulsates within me

***

A secret friend

There are troubling moments that can upset life
but it is in these moments that silence reveals itself
I close my eyes and feel
So I trust in the Divine again

***

Only in absolute silence, where no sound is heard or
spoken, dwells my truth.

***

In the sublime presence of silence, the true form of
nature is revealed.

***

In my hidden place

This is the place to which
I retire to restore my energies
where with closed eyes
I attain seclusion and know peace

***

Why so much discord?

91

Fighting for one thing…
Protesting for another…
Our essence knows no such contradictions
Our essence is simplicity and gentleness

***

The most beautiful spectacle

In the enchanting sky
clouds pass by
in their honey-colored robes
It is twilight
It is time for divine art
I wish to lie down in the warm sand
by the sea of Beauty
and ponder this wonder

***

A little closer to myself

I can see with the eyes of the heart
or with the eyes of matter
That sometimes we make good choices
but there is a place from which they emanate
It is this temple that I enter
when I am in contact with myself
without judgment

***

While I meditate
I feel a certain spiritual support
I feel that I am not alone
I have never been

***

The more I meditate
the more I discover myself
The more I love
The more I reinvent myself

***

Every time I meditate
angels gather in my pocket
and dance and sing with much joy
That is why
when I open my eyes
after my silence
I open a beautiful smile

***

The manuscript

A flickering manuscript vibrates in my heart. Whenever I want to read it, I retreat to a quiet place. I close my eyes and focus my attention on the third eye, the point between my eyebrows. There I surrender to silence.
Like dripping drops of water, I gradually unravel the lines of this great book.

***

Under the sky, I have only one goal:
"to know myself."
So why do I run so fast
to grab what is not mine?

***

An unusual visit

I once met the Soul in a dream. We were sitting around a campfire on the top of a mountain. It said to me:

"I, your eternal companion, free, silent, and joyful, always walk beside you with serenity, loving and serving you, even though I am master of myself, and you are slave to yourself. I walk beside you like a breeze beside the wind. I sing to you the sweet melody of the divine spring, a joy for beings aware of the present moment, and an infinite delight for loving hearts."

A golden ray invaded my room and landed on my pillow. My head felt delightfully caressed. Then I opened my eyes. The day began well.

***

The message from my heart

"Oh, old soul, eternity is nothing but a child by your side. I am Love, your only friend in this treacherous world where forgetfulness is your greatest enemy. When the sky falls to earth and the oceans cover life, remember me. I am the pulse of your body, and my presence by your side is a delight for the spirit, an endless bliss for those who love the Truth."

***

Solitude

This loneliness that haunts me like an evil thought can only be a delusion.
I am not alone.
I am aware that the absolute void is beside me.
I cannot see it, but I feel it.
This emptiness is everything and nothing at the same time.
I hear it, just as I hear the beating of my heart.
It makes no sound, and yet, it is the ultimate sound.
Through it, I perceive the many voices of the world.
I see them flowing pleasantly into me like the waves of the ocean, whispering their sweet melody in my ear.
Like the song of the divine dawn or the poetry of a loving being.
It must be the music that makes the rivers dance on their way to the sea.
It is the voice that releases the lotus from the swamp.
Varied as the buzzing of bees.
Delightful as the sound of a divine flute.
This supreme symphony kindled the sacred fire in my heart, and I have known the joy of love ever since.

***

O Soul

Beautiful Soul, clothed in man, hear the groaning of your heart, which is tormented by the garment.

Radiant Soul, without color, sex, or race, love yourself, for in your heart is kept the Truth of truths.

Ancient Soul, love the Creation, the only and sublime Truth which is beyond the horizons.

Merciful Soul, love your fellow beings, for they are the tiny particles of your being.

Caring Soul, love, respect, organize, protect, and harmonize yourself with nature, which is your Great Mother in this transient world.

***

We hope you enjoy the reading.
For more phrases like these,
Please follow our posts on Instagram:
@herlicpoemas

Thank you!